Giants on the Road

Ambulances

Norman D. Graubart

PowerKiDS press.

New York

Published in 2015 by The Rosen Publishing Group, Inc.
29 East 21st Street, New York, NY 10010

First Edition

Editor: Katie Kawa
Book Design: Jonathan J. D'Rozario

Photo Credits: Cover Robert Asento/Shutterstock.com; back cover Photoraidz/Shutterstock.com; pp. 5, 24 (hospital) I. Pilon/Shutterstock.com; p. 6 Bryant Jayme/Shutterstock.com; p. 9 thelefty/Shutterstock.com; pp. 10, 24 (EMT) Tyler Olson/Shutterstock.com; p. 13 Cavan Images/Iconica/Getty Images; pp. 14, 24 (siren) Glen Jones/ Shutterstock.com; p. 17 George Doyle/ Stockbyte/Thinkstock.com; p. 18 Dennis O'Clair/Getty Images; p. 21 TIM MCCAIG/iStock/Thinkstock.com; p. 22 View Apart/Shutterstock.com.

Library of Congress Cataloging-in-Publication Data

Graubart, Norman D., author.
 Ambulances / Norman D. Graubart.
     pages cm. — (Giants on the road)
 Includes bibliographical references and index.
 ISBN 978-1-4994-0030-4 (pbk.)
 ISBN 978-1-4994-0032-8 (6 pack)
 ISBN 978-1-4994-0029-8 (library binding)
 1. Ambulances—Juvenile literature. I. Title.
 TL235.8.G735 2015
 629.222'34—dc23
                                                        2014025278

Manufactured in the United States of America

CPSIA Compliance Information: Batch #CW15PK: For Further Information contact Rosen Publishing, New York, New York at 1-800-237-9932

Contents

Ambulances take people to the **hospital**.

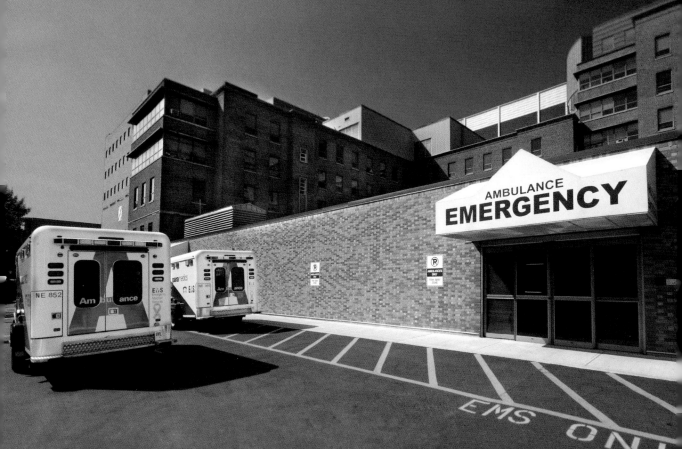

5

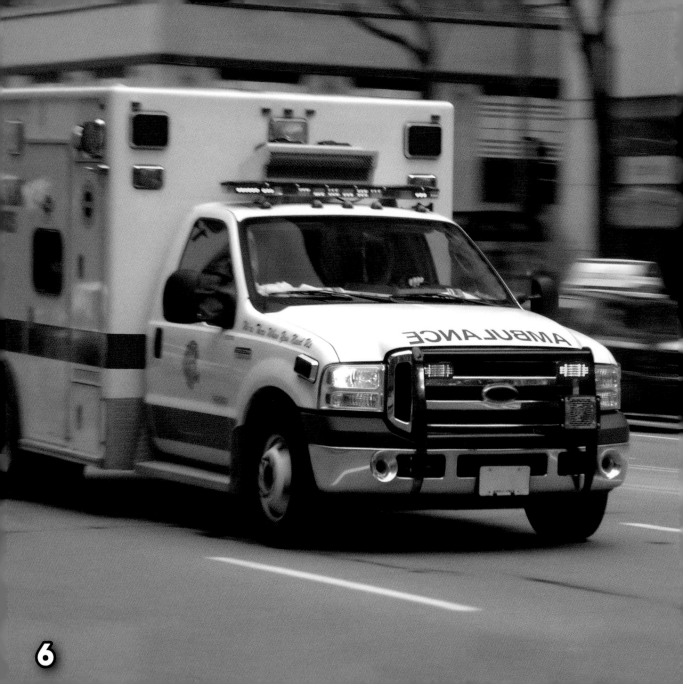

Ambulances are allowed
to drive very fast!

Ambulances carry things to help people who are sick or hurt.

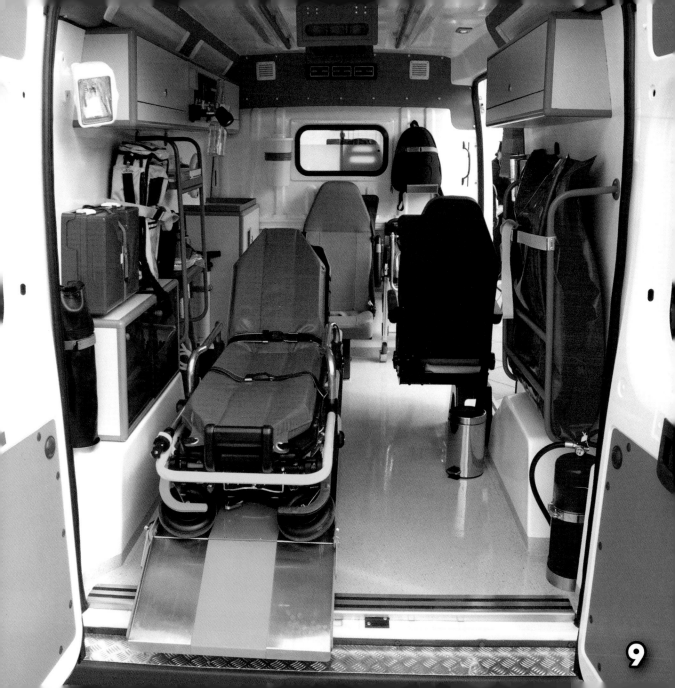

Workers called **EMTs** ride in ambulances.

EMTs make people feel better.
They also save lives!

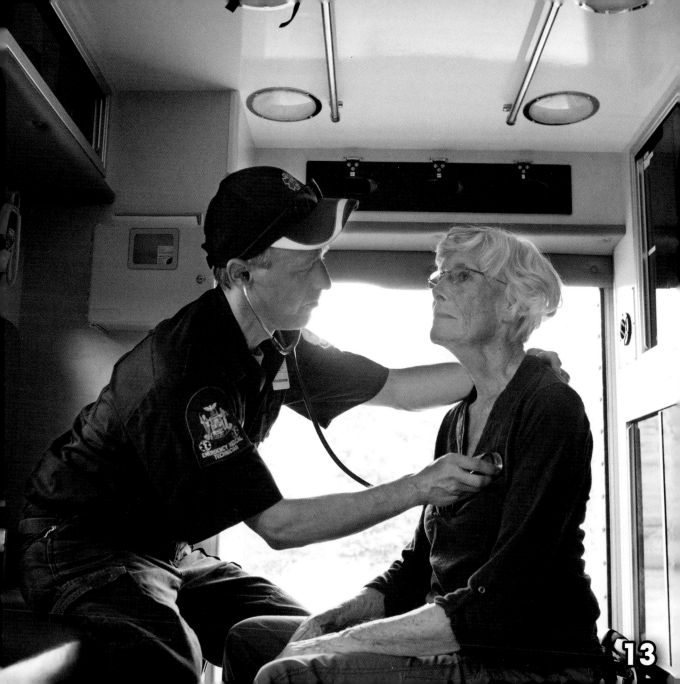

Ambulances have a **siren**.
Sirens are very loud!

Ambulances also have
red and white lights.

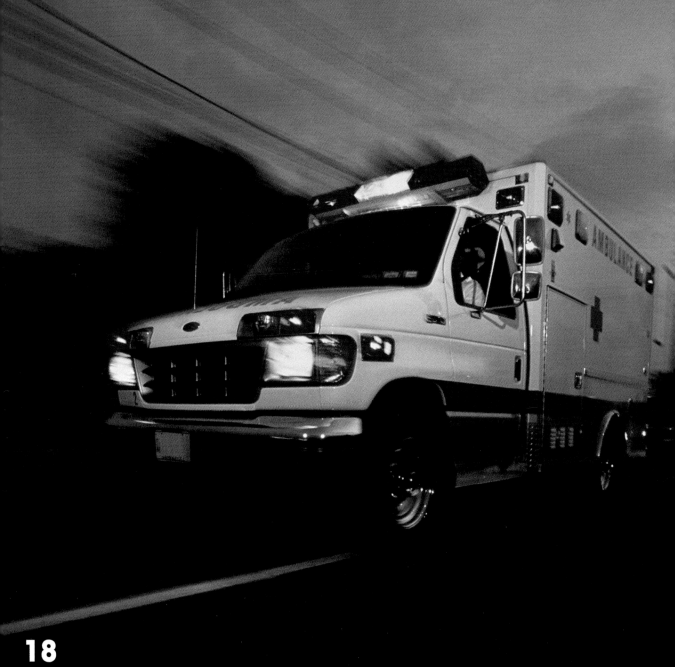

The siren and lights tell drivers an ambulance is on the road.

Other drivers must stop and let ambulances drive past them.

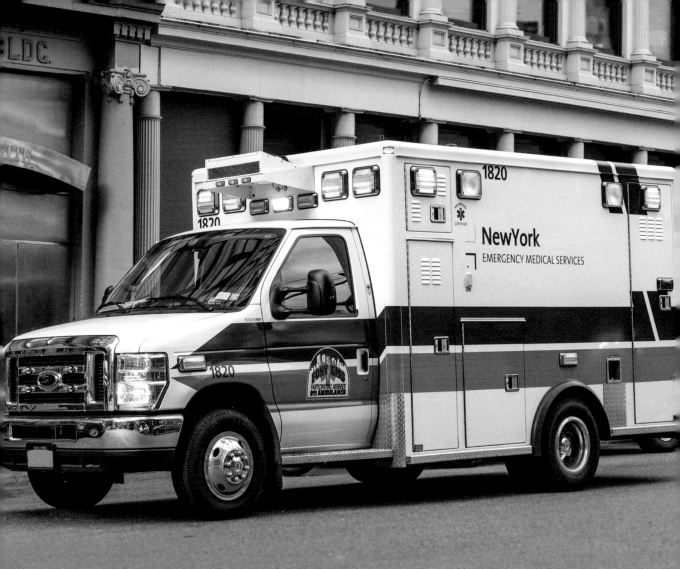

What else do you know
about ambulances?

Words to Know

EMTs

hospital

siren

Index

Websites

Due to the changing nature of Internet links, PowerKids Press has developed an online list of websites related to the subject of this book. This site is updated regularly. Please use this link to access the list: www.powerkidslinks.com/gotr/ambu